A Trip to Egypt

Chapter 4
Lesson 61: Decoding Skill 1
Lexile® Measure: 590L

Printed in the United States of America

Copyright © September 2012 by Reading Horizons

ISBN 978-1-62382-025-1

Levi and Elaine went on a trip to Egypt.
Before they left, they packed their bags.
They packed clothes and a first aid kit.
They packed pills in case they got sick.
They also packed things to read.

The flight to Egypt was very long.
To pass the time, they napped and
read. They even got to see a show
on the plane.

After they landed, an old man named
Simon picked them up in a green jeep.

The hot sun was shining. They drove
over a lot of sand and hills to a big,
cement hotel. Along the way, there were
many locusts hopping on the sand.

When they got to the hotel, they unpacked their bags and had a nap. Levi and Elaine decided it was wise to rest before sightseeing.

The next day, Levi and Elaine wanted to see a shrine. They asked Simon to drive them to see King Tut's grave site. It was a delight to see King Tut's gold mask.

On Friday, Simon drove Elaine and Levi
to see the Nile.

They saw where the Nile streams into the Mediterranean Sea. They saw people scuba diving. They looked for strange fish in the water. Then they went back to the hotel.

This was a great trip for Elaine and Levi!

The End

Comprehension Questions

1. This story is about
    a. a vacation.
    b. how to travel safely.
    c. where you should go if you visit Egypt.

2. The hotel that Levi and Elaine stayed in was made of
    a. sand.
    b. twigs.
    c. cement.

3. Where would a person most likely go sightseeing?
    a. in a movie theater
    b. in their own house
    c. in a place that someone is visiting for the first time

4. When Elaine and Levi got home from their trip, they were probably

    a. mad.

    b. confused.

    c. tired, but happy.

5. Which is one of the things that Simon showed Levi and Elaine?

    a. Disneyland

    b. King Tut's grave site

    c. The Tower of London

Skill Words

Levi	locusts
Elaine	decided
Egypt	delight
before*	Friday
even*	scuba
Simon	
over*	
cement	
hotel	

Most Common Words

a	great	on	this
after	had	over*	time
also	in	people	to
an	into	read	up
and	it	see	very
asked	landed	show	wanted
back	long	the	was
before*	looked	their	water
big	man	them	way
day	many	then	went
even*	named	there	were
first	of	they	when
for	old	things	where

Challenge Words

clothes
along
sightseeing
saw
Mediterranean

*both Skill Word and Most Common Word